Book of Mormon Family Night

Lessons That Teach with Treats

by
Cindy S. Pedersen

Illustrated by
Val Chadwick Bagley

Covenant Communications, Inc.

For Go-Go, My LadyBug,

and NickyBoat. I love you guys!

94 95 96 97 98 99 00   10 9 8 7 6 5 4 3 2 1

Book of Mormon Family Night, Lessons That Teach with Treats
Cover Design & Illustrations by Val Bagley
Covenant Communications, Inc.
ISBN 1-55503-761-5

Introduction

You're faced with another family home evening, another lesson. You want to make the lesson extra-special, to help involve your children, to help them remember. What can you do?

This book is filled with quick and easy ideas for fun treats that are easy to make and delicious to eat. Each treat is tied to a lesson from the scriptures to help your children better remember the lesson.

Even better, these recipes won't exclude your youngest children! All family members can be involved, from the toddler who loves to help pour in the ingredients, to the eight-year-old who can read the recipe or scripture story out loud, to the teenager who never refuses goodies, to the mom and dad who don't have a lot of time to prepare for family home evening. Older children can help younger brothers and sisters, and parents can finally get their children's attention while they're teaching them gospel principles and scripture stories.

Here's how to use this book:

1. Pick a Book of Mormon story that you'd like to teach, or use the lessons in the order they appear in this book.

2. Turn to the corresponding recipe. Collect the ingredients, gather the family together, and have a prayer to start your family night. Begin making the treat, having family members help wherever possible.

3. While you're making the goodies or waiting for them to cook, read the scripture story summary provided, look up the scripture reference, and read the story or tell it in your own words. (Parents may wish to adapt the story depending on the ages of the children involved. For instance, the burning and persecution of the righteous as related in the book of Alma may be disturbing to young children.)

4. Now, discuss the scripture story to make it stick in the kids' minds. The discussion questions are provided to help children remember the details of the scripture event—what the character learned, what you can learn from the story, and how you can apply what you've learned to your life. These aids help children make sense of why we need to read the Book of Mormon.

5. Share your own experiences relating to the scripture story, or have your kids share an experience. Take time to talk about your experiences and answer questions.

6. Have fun together as a family as you're learning and eating! Even if the recipes don't turn out exactly right, let your children have fun and experiment.

I hope you enjoy this book and find it useful in your quest to have quality, fun, delicious family time while teaching the scripture stories to your children. Remember, children learn better when you TEACH WITH TREATS!

TABLE OF CONTENTS

Sacred Grove Gumdrop Trees

This treat represents that sacred place where Joseph Smith knelt and asked which church was the correct one. In the grove, Joseph Smith saw and talked with Jesus Christ and Heavenly Father.

STORY: Joseph Smith History 1:5-20. When Joseph Smith was 14 years old, he did not know which church to join. One day as he was reading in the Bible, he read James 1:5, which said, "If any of you lack wisdom, let him ask of God, that giveth to all men liberally and upbraideth not; and it shall be given him."

This scripture touched him deeply, for he knew he needed help from God to make the right choice. The next day he went into the woods near his home to pray, and he knelt down within a grove of trees to ask God what he should do. Suddenly, he saw a bright light, and in the light were Heavenly Father and Jesus Christ. Heavenly Father pointed to Jesus and said, "This is my Son." Joseph asked which church he should join. Jesus Christ told him not to join any of them, for none of the churches on the earth were correct.

The place where Joseph witnessed Heavenly Father and Jesus Christ is known as the Sacred Grove.

DISCUSSION QUESTIONS
1. Why did Joseph Smith go into the woods to pray?
2. What happened?
3. What should you do if you need help making an important decision?
4. Have you ever prayed to know if the Church was true?
   (If you wish, share your experience of how you gained your testimony.)

RECIPE
4 c. original Cheerios
3 c. mini marshmallows
3 Tbsp. butter
1/2 tsp. vanilla
1/2 tsp. green food color
Small candies

On low heat, melt marshmallows and butter in medium saucepan until marshmallows melt. Remove from heat. Add vanilla and food color, stirring until smooth. Add Cheerios and stir until all the cereal is coated with marshmallow mixture.

Coat hands with butter or non-stick cooking spray, or simply wet hands. Use about 2/3 cup mixture for each tree. On greased cookie sheet or waxed paper, shape each portion into a pine tree (triangle) shape. To decorate, stick red hots, chocolate chips, gum drops, or any other candies you desire onto the trees. Makes approximately 16 trees.

Gather everyone's tree around in a circle and read Joseph Smith's first vision as the treats cool.

Hill Cumorah Dessert
(Some of this will need to be prepared ahead of time.)

The "hill" you make with this dessert will help to teach your family about why the Hill Cumorah is so important; for when they cut into it, there is a treasure inside, representing the treasure Joseph Smith was led to: the Golden Plates.

STORY: Joseph Smith History 1:28-53. Three years had passed since Joseph had visited the sacred grove, and he had been persecuted because of his vision. One night he knelt down and prayed, because he wanted to know what he should do. Suddenly, there was a bright light in his room, and in the light was an angel named Moroni. At first Joseph was afraid, but Moroni told him that God had a great work for him to do, and he was no longer fearful. Moroni also told Joseph about a book, hidden under a big rock in the Hill Cumorah, that was a history of people who lived in America many years ago. The book was about the gospel of Jesus Christ.

Joseph went to the hill and moved the rock. He found the book in a stone box. The book's pages were made of gold, and they had writing on them in a different language than we use. Moroni wouldn't let Joseph take the gold plates at that time. He told Joseph to come back each year, and after four years, he let Joseph take the plates.

DISCUSSION QUESTIONS
1. What was buried in the Hill Cumorah?
2. How did Joseph find this out?
3. Why wouldn't the angel Moroni let Joseph take the plates right away?
4. How long did Joseph wait before he was able to take the golden plates with him to translate them?

RECIPE
2 pints or 1 quart of your favorite ice cream
1 1-inch-thick piece of sponge cake or layer cake
5 egg whites
3/4 tsp. vanilla
1/2 tsp. cream of tartar
2/3 c. sugar

Soften ice cream by microwaving it for 1 minute or leaving it out at room temperature for 15 minutes. Stir ice cream into a mixing bowl with a diameter 2 inches smaller than the diameter of the cake. Smooth out the top of ice cream in bowl. Cover and freeze until ice cream is very firm (about 1 hour).

Dip bowl in hot water for 10 seconds so that ice cream will slide easily out of the bowl onto the cake. Place cake on foil and center ice cream on top. Cover and freeze until firm.

About 10 minutes before serving time, preheat oven to 500°. Make meringue to go over the top by beating egg whites, cream of tartar, and vanilla until soft peaks form. Add sugar, 1 Tbsp. at a time, beating until stiff peaks form.

On a baking sheet, center cake with ice cream, then spread with meringue, being certain to seal around the edges of the cake and baking sheet. Swirl meringue around with a spatula to make pretty peaks, then bake for about 3 minutes or until golden. After everyone has admired the dessert, slice and serve immediately. Serves 8.

Urim and Thummim Treats

Use this treat to help take the mystery out of the Urim and Thummim, to help explain what it looked like, and to show how Joseph Smith used it.

STORY: Joseph Smith History 1:35. The angel Moroni told Joseph Smith about two stones in silver bows fastened to a breastplate, which was hidden with the gold plates in the Hill Cumorah. This was called the Urim and Thummim and was used by Joseph Smith for translating the gold plates into a language we can read and understand.

DISCUSSION QUESTIONS
1. What does the Urim and Thummim look like?
2. What did Joseph Smith use the Urim and Thummim to do?

RECIPE
Graham cracker for each serving
1/4 c. chocolate chips for each serving
2 large marshmallows for each serving
Peanut butter

Spread a thin layer of peanut butter over the graham cracker. Add chocolate chips in rows to create decorations on the "breastplate." Put one large marshmallow on each half of graham cracker for each part of the Urim and Thummim stones. Cook in microwave oven for about 35 seconds, or until the marshmallows melt.

To cook in conventional oven: put on cookie sheet and cook at 500° for about 3 minutes. Be sure to watch closely and take out when toasty brown!

Tower of Babel Cake

Just as the wicked people of Babel built a tower to try and get to heaven, so will you build a "tower" with pieces of Devil's Food Cake.

STORY: Ether 1:33 and Genesis 11. Jared and his brother lived in a place called Babel. Many wicked people also lived there. The wicked people built a tower, called the Tower of Babel, to get to heaven. This made God angry.

God changed the language of the wicked people so that they all used different words. They couldn't understand each other.

The brother of Jared was a good man who obeyed God. He prayed and asked God not to change the language of his family and friends, who were called Jaredites. God didn't change their language because they were righteous and because Jared had prayed to Him.

DISCUSSION QUESTIONS
1. Why did the wicked people of Babel build a tower?
2. How do you think God felt about this?
3. How do we get to heaven?
4. What did God do to the wicked people?
5. Who was righteous and living in Babel?

RECIPE
(This can be just as effective using a Devil's Food cake mix and pre-bought frosting.)
2 1/4 c. flour
1/2 c. unsweetened cocoa
1 1/2 tsp. baking soda
1/2 tsp. salt
1/2 c. shortening
1 c. sugar

1 tsp. vanilla
3 egg yolks
1 1/3 c. cold water
3 egg whites
3/4 c. sugar

Beat shortening on medium speed in large mixing bowl for about 30 seconds. Add 1 cup sugar and the vanilla, then beat until fluffy. Add the egg yolks, one at a time, beating after each. Add flour, cocoa, baking soda, salt, and water, beating on low speed until mixed.

Beat egg whites in a small mixing bowl until soft peaks form, then slowly add 3/4 cup sugar, 1 Tbsp. at a time, beating until stiff peaks form and sugar is dissolved.

Fold egg mixture into batter, combining well, but do not beat. Turn batter into 13x9x2-inch greased and floured pan. Bake in 350° oven for 30-35 minutes. Cool 20 minutes and cut into 3x3-inch squares.

Frosting
1 c. sugar
1/4 tsp. cream of tartar
1/3 c. water
2 egg whites
1 tsp. vanilla
Dash salt

Combine sugar, cream of tartar, salt, and 1/3 cup water in saucepan, cooking until it boils and sugar is dissolved.

Combine egg whites and vanilla in a mixing bowl, then add sugar syrup VERY SLOWLY to unbeaten egg whites while beating at high speed. Continue beating about 7 minutes or until stiff peaks form.

If desired, add red food color to frosting.

NOW THE FUN BEGINS: Have each family member wash their hands, then give them several pieces of cake and put the frosting bowl where everyone can reach it. Place a cookie sheet in the middle of the group, and have each family member stack one piece of cake on top of another to build your own "tower," adding frosting between each layer. Tell the story of the "Tower of Babel," and when your own tower collapses, gather up the pieces and eat as you tell the rest of the story.

Brother of Jared Thumbprint Stone Cookies

With these cookies, you can show what can happen if you have faith. When the brother of Jared gathered the small, white stones, he had faith enough to see the finger of the Lord as He touched them, making them glow to give the Jaredites light for their long journey.

STORY: Ether 1:38–6:12. God told the Jaredites he would lead them to a promised land, so they left their homes, gathered their flocks of animals, and went to the sea. For a long time, the brother of Jared didn't pray. Jesus told him to repent and pray often, so he repented and Jesus forgave him.

Jesus then told the brother of Jared to build some boats to take them to the promised land. He obeyed, and the Jaredites built eight small boats that were shaped like a dish on all sides, according to the directions given to them by the Lord. When the boats were finished, the brother of Jared told Jesus there was no light in the boats to see as they were traveling. Jesus told him to think of a way to bring light into the boats.

The brother of Jared thought and thought, then gathered 16 small, white stones. He took the stones to the top of a mountain and prayed, asking Jesus to touch these stones with his finger to make them shine. Jesus reached out his finger and touched the stones to make them shine. The brother of Jared had faith in Jesus Christ, so he saw Jesus' finger. Because he had great faith, he saw that Jesus had a body.

The brother of Jared put two stones in each boat for light. The Jaredites climbed in the boats, and after many days, they arrived in the promised land. They thanked God for helping them arrive safely.

DISCUSSION QUESTIONS
1. What did the brother of Jared do when the wicked people of Babel's language was being changed?
2. What did God tell him to do?
3. What did the brother of Jared do wrong that Jesus Christ told him to repent of?
4. How did the brother of Jared get light into the boats?
5. What did the people do when they arrived in the promised land?

RECIPE
1 c. butter
1/3 c. granulated sugar
2 tsp. vanilla
2 c. flour
1/4 c. powdered sugar
1 can prepared lemon pie filling

Beat butter for 30 seconds; add sugar and beat until fluffy. Add vanilla and 2 tsp. water. Beat well. Stir in flour. Shape into 1-inch balls. Place on an ungreased cookie sheet. Press down centers with thumb. Bake in a 325° oven about 18 minutes. Cool completely. Gently shake a few cookies at a time in a bag with powdered sugar. Fill hollow with prepared lemon pie filling. Makes 36.

Lehi's Altar of Scones

When Lehi and his family were warned by Heavenly Father to leave Jerusalem, they did. After three days, Lehi built an altar of stones and prayed to give his thanks to the Lord.

STORY: 1 Nephi 1:2-7. Lehi and his family lived near Jerusalem 600 years before Jesus Christ was born. Lehi's wife's name was Sariah, and they had four sons: Laman, Lemuel, Sam, and Nephi. They lived in Jerusalem, where many people were wicked. God sent prophets to tell the wicked people to repent, but they wouldn't listen.

One night Lehi had a vision. In the vision, God told Lehi Jerusalem would be destroyed. Lehi told the people to repent, telling them about his vision, but the wicked people didn't believe him and they were very angry. Some even tried to kill him. So God spoke to Lehi in a dream and told him to leave Jerusalem.

Lehi and his family obeyed God and went into the wilderness. Laman and Lemuel didn't want to leave Jerusalem, but Nephi and Sam obeyed Lehi, for they believed what he had told them.

After three days, they came to a river and put up their tents. Lehi built an altar of stones and thanked God for helping them.

DISCUSSION QUESTIONS
1. Why did Lehi and his family leave Jerusalem?
2. How did his family feel about this?
3. What did Lehi do after three days in the wilderness?
4. Why did he do this?

5. How do we thank God for all we have?

RECIPE
Make your favorite roll dough or use the following:
1 container pre-made biscuit dough
oil
Favorite toppings: honey, jam, syrup, fruit, powdered sugar, granulated
sugar, etc.

Heat oil to 375°. Carefully add 2-3 biscuits. Fry until brown on one side, then turn over to cook other side. Drain on plate with paper towels underneath. When ready to serve, stack in a pile, like the altar Lehi built. Then tell the story as your family digs in, topping the scones with whatever toppings they wish. Makes 10 scones.

Brass Plates Cake

God sent Nephi and his brothers back to Jerusalem to get the brass plates from Laban. The brass plates were important because they contained a record of Lehi's ancestors. This treat can teach the importance of keeping records, even today.

STORY: 1 Nephi 3–5. The brass plates were a book that the prophets had written upon. The plates were filled with stories of Adam and Eve and Moses. They were also a record of people in Lehi's family who lived long ago. It was very important for Lehi's family to have the brass plates, so God told Lehi to have Nephi and his brothers go back to Jerusalem to get the plates from a man named Laban.

Laman and Lemuel didn't want to go to Jerusalem to get the plates. They were angry because their father made them go. But Nephi knew God would help them and prepare a way for them to get the plates.

Laman went to Laban's house and asked him for the brass plates. But Laban would not give him the brass plates. He was angry and said he would kill Laman.

Laman was afraid, and he ran back to his brothers. He told them he wanted to go back into the wilderness. But Nephi said they must obey God and get the brass plates. So they went to their old home near Jerusalem to get their gold and silver and precious things to buy the brass plates.

Laban was happy to take their gold and silver, but he still wouldn't give them the brass plates. In fact, he told his men to kill Lehi's sons! So they ran away and hid in a cave, leaving their precious things behind.

DISCUSSION QUESTIONS
1. Why did Lehi send Nephi, Sam, Laman, and Lemuel back to Jerusalem?
2. Did Laman and Lemuel want to go?
3. Did Laban give the plates to them?
4. Why were the brass plates so important to have?
5. Are you keeping your own record, or journal?
6. What did Lehi's sons decide to do after Laban wouldn't give the plates to them?

RECIPE
(NOTE: This can also be made using a yellow cake mix.)
2 c. flour
2 1/2 tsp. baking powder
1/2 tsp. salt
2/3 c. shortening
1 1/2 c. sugar
1 Tbsp. grated orange peel
1 1/2 tsp. grated lemon peel
3 eggs
2/3 c. milk
2 Tbsp. lemon juice
Can of lemon pie filling
Fluffy White Frosting
Chocolate chips or lemon gumdrops

In a large mixing bowl, beat shortening about 30 seconds, then add sugar, peels, and eggs, beating well. Add flour, baking powder, salt, milk, and lemon juice until well blended. Turn into a 13x9x2-inch pan. Bake in a 350° oven for 30 minutes or until done. Cool. Remove from pan.

Cut cake in half, making 2 cake layers the same size (or book size). Spread lemon pie filling on one layer, then stack the second layer on top so they are the same size and shape as a book. Frost top and sides with Fluffy White Frosting (see frosting recipe for Tower of Babel Cake, p. 6) colored with yellow food color. On top, write "The Brass Plates" with chocolate chips or lemon gumdrops.

Sword of Laban Breadstick Treats

When Nephi came upon the drunken form of Laban, God told Nephi to kill him. At first, Nephi resisted. Then God told Nephi that sometimes it's better for one person to die than for an entire nation to lose its sacred records. Nephi obeyed God and cut off Laban's head with Laban's sword.

STORY: 1 Nephi 3:28-4:34. When Lehi's sons got to the cave after running away from Laban, Laman and Lemuel were angry with Nephi and their father. They beat Nephi and Sam with a stick. Suddenly, an angel of God appeared and asked them why they were hitting their brothers. He said God would help them get the brass plates, but they needed to obey Nephi.

After the angel left, Laman and Lemuel continued to complain, but they went along anyway, hiding outside the wall while the Holy Ghost led Nephi to Laban's house. As Nephi approached, he saw a man near Laban's house. Nephi came closer and saw that it was Laban. Laban was very drunk. The Holy Ghost told Nephi to kill Laban so that Nephi's family could obtain the brass plates. They would need the brass plates to help them learn about the gospel. Nephi didn't want to kill Laban, but he knew he had to get the brass plates for his family. Nephi took Laban's sword and cut off Laban's head with it.

Nephi then put on Laban's clothes and went into Laban's house, where he met Laban's servant, Zoram. Zoram thought Nephi was Laban, so when Nephi told Zoram to bring the brass plates and follow him, Zoram obeyed.

DISCUSSION QUESTIONS
1. Who stopped Laman and Lemuel from beating Nephi?
2. What did Nephi do after the angel came?
3. Who told Nephi to kill Laban?
4. Did Nephi want to kill Laban?

5. How did Nephi get the brass plates?

RECIPE
(You can also use your favorite bread recipe.)
3 c. flour
1/2 c. sugar
3 tsp. salt
1 Tbsp. oil
3 c. VERY HOT water
2 Tbsp. yeast
1/3 c. powdered milk
3 eggs
2 Tbsp. potato flakes
Butter or margarine
Cinnamon and sugar mixture
Maraschino Cherries
Powdered sugar icing

Mix all dry ingredients together thoroughly. Add HOT water (as hot as you can get from the tap). Mix. Add the rest of the ingredients and mix. Add enough flour to form a good dough (about 2-3 more cups). Turn out onto lightly floured surface, and knead in enough flour to make a moderately stiff dough that is smooth and elastic (6-8 minutes total). Shape into a ball. Place in a greased bowl. Turn once. Cover and let rise in a warm place until double (45-60 minutes).

Punch down, and turn out onto a lightly floured surface. Divide in half and roll out one of the pieces with a rolling pin until dough is about 1 inch thick. Cut 8x2-inch pieces. Two inches from the bottom, set a piece of dough 2x1-inch right above where the handle of the sword is going to be. If you desire, cut the area below this into 3 pieces and braid, pinching together at the end. Brush with some melted butter and sprinkle with cinnamon and sugar. Decorate with cherries as rubies. Let rise until double (about 30 minutes). Bake in 375º oven for 10-15 minutes. Drizzle with icing.

Powdered Sugar Icing
1 c. powdered sugar
1/4 tsp. vanilla
Milk

In a mixing bowl, stir together powdered sugar, vanilla, and enough milk to make of drizzling consistency (about 1 1/2 Tbsp.).

Lehi's Fruit of the Tree

In Lehi's dream, he saw a tree with fruit that was delicious above all others, signifying God's love.

STORY: 1 Nephi 8:2-35. Lehi had a dream in which he saw a man in a white robe. This man led Lehi to a tree after he had spent many hours in darkness. Lehi ate the white fruit off the tree, and it filled him with great joy. After he ate the fruit, he saw Sariah, his wife, and Sam and Nephi standing at the head of a river. They looked as if they didn't know where to go, so Lehi called to them and they came. They followed the river and the rod of iron that led to the tree. Like Lehi, they ate the fruit.

Lehi also called to Laman and Lemuel, but they would not come. There was a large field where many people were gathered, pressing forward to find the tree. A mist of darkness caused many of the people to lose their way. Others caught hold of the iron rod, which led them to the tree.

On the other side of the river was a large building filled with all kinds of people dressed in fine clothing. These people were pointing their fingers and making fun of those who ate the fruit.

Lehi saw many who made their way to the building. Others got caught in the fountain of water and were drowned.

DISCUSSION QUESTIONS
1. Where did Lehi see the Tree of Life?
2. What else did he see in his vision?
3. What did each of those things mean?
4. Is it easy to follow the straight and narrow path when it feels like the world is laughing at you?
   (Share an experience when it was hard to do the right thing.)

RECIPE
6 tart red apples
6 caramels
24 mini marshmallows
6 tsp. raisins
3 tsp. coconut (optional)

Vanilla ice cream

Wash apples and core, leaving 1/2 inch on the bottom, and leaving a hole in the top 1 1/2 inches across. Give each family member an apple to place on a square of aluminum foil, and let them fill the apple's hole with 4 marshmallows, 1 caramel, 1 tsp. raisins, and 1/2 tsp. coconut. Seal each apple in aluminum foil, and cook at 350° in a 13x9x2-inch pan for 45-60 minutes. As you unwrap the fruit dessert, watch out for the steam!

Serve on a plate with a scoop of vanilla ice cream. Serves 6.

Liahona Carmel Popcorn Balls

After going into the wilderness, Lehi found an unusual brass ball outside his tent. He called it the Liahona. It was like a compass, and it showed them the way to go if they were righteous. These edible balls will help to teach your family what the Liahona might have looked like.

STORY: 1 Nephi 16: 9-32. After Nephi and his brothers went back to Jerusalem once more to get Ishmael and his family, God told Lehi to go farther into the wilderness. One day, Lehi was surprised to find a strange ball outside his tent. It was round and made of fine brass, and within it were two spindles, one of which pointed the way to go. It was called the Liahona, and it only pointed the way to go if the people obeyed God. If they didn't obey God, the Liahona did not work.

DISCUSSION QUESTIONS
1. What did Lehi find outside his tent?
2. What did the Liahona do?
3. When did it work?
4. When didn't it work?
5. What would it be like to have something that pointed the way we should go in our lives? (We do! The scriptures.)

RECIPE
2 c. brown sugar
1 c. white Karo syrup
1/2 c. butter
1 can sweetened condensed milk

20 large gumdrops
20 toothpicks
20 1x1-inch paper arrows made out of any color construction paper

Mix brown sugar and Karo syrup in medium saucepan and bring to a boil. Add butter and melt. Mix in sweetened condensed milk and vanilla. Cook to a soft ball stage. Pour over 8 quarts popcorn, mixing thoroughly. Butter hands and shape into balls. Let the balls cool for 10 minutes, then stick a toothpick into the top of each one. Put a paper arrow on the toothpick and a gumdrop on top. Makes 20 balls.

Nephi's Banana Boat

Nephi didn't know how to make a ship to take him and his family to the promised land, but by listening to Heavenly Father, he learned how. In the same way, your family doesn't know how to make this dessert until they listen carefully as you tell them.

STORY: 1 Nephi 17-18. One day, God told Nephi to build a ship to carry him and his family to the promised land. Nephi didn't know how to build the ship, but he made tools and trusted in God, and God told him how to do it.

Laman and Lemuel didn't believe God told Nephi to build a ship, so they refused to work. Nephi told Laman and Lemuel they should repent and obey because he knew that God would help them. This made Laman and Lemuel angry, and they tried to throw Nephi into the sea, but the power of God was with him. God told Nephi to touch Laman and Lemuel and when he touched them, God shook them so that they knew, without a doubt, that God was helping Nephi. Nephi then told them to repent and obey God and their parents.

Because they were afraid, Laman and Lemuel repented and helped Nephi build the ship. When Nephi needed help, he asked God and God taught him how to build the ship. At last the ship was finished.

The family loaded the ship and climbed aboard. For many days the wind blew them towards the promised land. Then Laman and Lemuel and Ishmael's sons got angry at Nephi because Nephi told them to obey God. They tied Nephi with ropes and wouldn't let him go. Because Laman and Lemuel were so wicked, the Liahona stopped working, so they didn't know which way to go.

Lehi, Sariah, and Nephi's wife and children begged Laman and Lemuel to untie Nephi, but they wouldn't listen. Because of their wickedness, a storm blew the ship backwards for three days. On the fourth day the storm became very bad, and the ship almost sank. Laman and Lemuel were afraid for their lives, and they knew God was angry, so they untied Nephi. Nephi picked up the Liahona and it worked again, pointing the way toward the promised land.

Nephi prayed, and the storm stopped. Then they were able to sail the ship to the promised land following the direction of the Liahona.

DISCUSSION QUESTIONS
1. Why did Nephi build a ship?

2. How did Nephi learn to make the ship?
3. What did Laman and Lemuel want to do to Nephi when they saw him building the ship?
4. What happened when they tried to throw Nephi into the sea?
5. Does the Lord protect those that are doing good works for him?
6. What did Laman and Lemuel do to Nephi on the ship?
7. What happened when they tied him up?

RECIPE
1/4 c. salted, chopped peanuts
4 large bananas
1 carton (4 1/2 ounces) frozen whipped topping, thawed
Chocolate syrup
Strawberry topping
4 maraschino cherries

Wash unpeeled bananas gently, then slit the top of each banana peel lengthwise, leaving 1 inch uncut at each end. With washed scissors, cut 1/2 inch of peel on each side. Scoop out banana in small pieces with teaspoon and put into bowl. Reserve shells. Fold banana pieces and whipped topping together.

Put 1/4 of banana mix into banana shell and drizzle with chocolate syrup and strawberry topping. Top with 1/4 cup of chopped peanuts and a cherry. Serve right away or refrigerate for up to one hour. Makes 4 servings.

Nephites' Graham Temples

Because the Nephites loved God, they built a temple where they could worship Him and be closer to Him.

STORY: 2 Nephi 5:9-16. After Lehi blessed his family and died, Laman and Lemuel became wicked. When Nephi told them to repent, they became angry and tried to kill him.

God told Nephi to flee into the wilderness away from his brothers. Nephi took Zoram, Sam, Jacob, Joseph, his sisters, and their families with him. They called themselves Nephites, and they were righteous people. They planted crops and worked hard.

Laman and Lemuel's people were called Lamanites, and God made their skin dark. They were wicked and would not work.

The Nephites loved God, and they built a temple like Solomon's temple. The temple didn't have as many precious things, though, because jewels and other precious things were not found on the land.

DISCUSSION QUESTIONS
1. What did Laman and Lemuel try to do to Nephi after Lehi died?
2. Where did Nephi go and who did he take with him?
3. What did Nephi's people call themselves?
4. What did Laman and Lemuel's people call themselves?
5. What did the Nephites build?
6. Why did they do this?

RECIPE
(It may be a little hard for small children to put the walls up for their own graham cracker "temple," but once the basic structure is up, kids are a natural to decorate them!)
3 graham crackers
Powdered sugar frosting (see sword of Laban Breadstick Treat, p. 13)
Little candies to decorate with: M&Ms, gumdrops, nuts, red hots, etc.

For each temple, break 3 graham crackers in half. Take 4 of those pieces and form a square, using the frosting as glue for the "walls." "Glue" one piece on top, directly over the square. Break the last piece in two and center these on top of the roof, standing upright, leaning against each other to form a spire. Now decorate however you wish and eat!

Enos' Marshmallow Forest

Enos teaches us the power and importance of prayer when he goes into the forest to pour his soul out to the Lord. Make your own "forest" out of these treats, and pray for something your family needs help with, or offer a prayer of thankfulness before you eat.

STORY: Enos 1:3-21. Jacob was Enos' father, and he had taught Enos to obey God. Enos wanted to be righteous like his father. One day he went to hunt animals in the forest, but instead he knelt down to pray and to talk to God. Enos prayed and prayed all day, and when night came, he was still praying.

Suddenly, Enos heard the voice of God. God told Enos his sins were forgiven because he had faith in Jesus Christ and had obeyed God's commandments.

Enos then prayed for the Nephites to be blessed. God told Enos He would bless the Nephites if they would obey His commandments.

Enos then prayed for the Lamanites, who had become wicked and fought with the Nephites continually. He prayed that what was written on the gold plates would help the Lamanites someday and that they would become a righteous people.

God promised Enos that He would keep the gold plates safe from harm and that the words on the gold plates would help the Lamanites some day. Enos then went home and told the people what God had said to him.

DISCUSSION QUESTIONS
1. Why did Enos go into the forest?
2. How long did he pray?
3. What did God tell him?
4. What did Enos do after God forgave him?
5. What did God promise Enos?
6. If we want to repent or ask God for help, what do we do?

RECIPE
4 c. cornflakes
3 c. marshmallows
1/4 c. butter
Green food color
Mini candy bars like Snickers, 100 Grand, or Milky Way

Tear off a long sheet of waxed paper, or tear individual pieces for each "tree." Melt butter on low heat. Add marshmallows and melt. Stir until smooth and remove from heat. Add food color. Stir in cornflakes until thoroughly covered. Coat hands with butter or non-stick cooking spray, or wet hands with water. Using about 3/4 cup of the mixture, shape into the top of a tree. Unwrap a mini candy bar and place underneath for the trunk of the tree.

King Benjamin's Pink Pancake Tower

King Benjamin made a tower so that he could stand tall enough to talk to his people before he died. You can make a "Pancake Tower" with your family and give the same important message.

STORY: Mosiah 1:9-5:6. King Benjamin was a good king who took care of the gold plates and worked hard with his people. He grew old and wanted to talk to all his people before he died, so he stood on a tower to address them. He said that they should always help each other and when they helped each other, they would help God. He also told them about Jesus Christ, the Son of God. King Benjamin taught that Jesus would come to earth and bless and teach the people, heal the sick, bring the dead people back to life, and make blind people to see and deaf people to hear.

King Benjamin said Jesus' mother's name would be Mary. He said that some wicked people would put Jesus on a cross and kill him. But after three days he would be resurrected and would come back to life. Jesus would die for our sins and if we repented, we could be forgiven of our sins.

The Nephites fell to the ground because they felt bad they had sinned and they wanted to repent. The Nephites prayed to be forgiven, and God forgave them. They were very happy and were filled with the Holy Ghost, and they promised to obey God's commandments.

King Benjamin was very happy, for the people had made the right choice in repenting and promising to obey God's commandments.

DISCUSSION QUESTIONS
1. Why did King Benjamin stand on a tower?
2. What did he tell his people?
3. How did the people react?
4. What did God do when the people did this?
5. Would you make a promise to keep the commandments?

RECIPE
1 1/2 c. prepared pancake batter (use the 12-16 pancake recipe)
1 pkg. (4-serving size) red Jello
1/2 c. chopped bananas

1/4 c. chopped nuts (optional)

Add all ingredients together and mix. Cook as directed on pancake batter mix. Stack into a "tower," then tell the story of King Benjamin as your family digs in. Top with whatever you wish: syrup, jam, whipped topping, etc.

Nephi's F

Abinadi's Repentance Cupcakes

Abinadi called King Noah's people to repentance because of their sins. These cupcakes are chocolate on the outside—dark, like sin. When we repent, we become like the inside of the cupcakes—pure and white.

STORY: Mosiah 11-17. A man named Noah became the Nephites' king. Noah was very wicked and didn't obey God's commandments. He never worked for what he got; he just made the people bring him money and gifts. He also chose wicked men to lead the church, and these men taught the people to sin.

God sent a prophet named Abinadi to the people, and Abinadi told the people they were wicked and they needed to repent or be punished.

King Noah didn't like what Abinadi was saying. He had his men tie Abinadi up and bring him to the king and his priests, who wanted to kill Abinadi. They asked Abinadi many questions, for they wanted to trick him into saying something wrong. But God blessed Abinadi, and he told Noah and his priests they were wicked.

The priests were very angry and tried to kill Abinadi, but they couldn't. God protected Abinadi because he had more for Abinadi to teach. Abinadi told the king and priests they would be punished if they didn't repent. He also told them about Jesus Christ and that they needed to obey God's commandments. He told the priests they needed to love God and teach the truth to help the people. But Noah and his priests wouldn't listen, and they sent Abinadi off to prison.

One of the priests believed Abinadi's words. His name was Alma. Because he believed Abinadi, Alma asked Noah to let Abinadi go. Noah didn't want to let Abinadi go, and he was very angry with Alma. He sent soldiers to kill him, but they couldn't catch him because Alma ran away and hid.

Three days later, Noah had Abinadi brought before him and told him that he should take back what he had said or else he would be killed. But Abinadi knew he had told the truth and would not change his words. So Noah told his soldiers to kill Abinadi by burning him to death. Abinadi was killed, but he was not afraid to die, for he was a righteous man who obeyed God.

DISCUSSION QUESTIONS
1. Was King Noah a good man?
2. Who did God send to King Noah and his people?
3. What did Abinadi tell them to do?
4. What happened when Noah's soldiers tried to kill Abinadi the first time?
5. Did any of the priests believe Abinadi?
6. What happened to Abinadi? Do you think he was afraid?

RECIPE
1 white cake mix
Ingredients for cake mix
Decorations like jelly beans, chocolate chips, or other candies

Make the cake batter; pour into cupcake liners and bake. Let cool about 20 minutes, then frost with frosting below. Kids love to help frost, even if it isn't done just right. Decorate with jelly beans or other candies.

Sinful Chocolate Frosting
6 Tbsp. butter, softened
4 1/2- 4 3/4 c. sifted powdered sugar
1/4 c. milk
1 1/2 tsp. vanilla
2 squares unsweetened chocolate, melted and cooled

Mix butter and 1/2 of powdered sugar in small mixing bowl. Beat well. Add milk, vanilla, and cooled, melted chocolate. Mix thoroughly, then gradually beat in the rest of the powdered sugar.

If necessary, you can add milk to make frosting of good spreading consistency.

King Limhi's Grape Escape Drink

King Limhi's people were captured by the Lamanites because they didn't listen to Abinadi and repent. In order to escape, they had to repent, then God helped them think of a way to escape. Wine is like the grape juice in this drink, only wine is fermented.

STORY: Mosiah 7, 21-22. King Noah had a son named Limhi who wasn't wicked like his father. He was a righteous king. Limhi's people were captured by the Lamanites because they had been wicked.

Limhi asked his people to come and listen to him. When they were gathered, he told them that the reason they had been captured was because they didn't listen to the prophet Abinadi when he told them to repent. Limhi then told his people that if they would repent, God would help them. The people repented and promised to obey God's commandments.

The Nephites then thought of a way to escape. They gave wine to the Lamanite soldiers, and the Lamanites became drunk from the wine and fell asleep. The Nephites then escaped from the drunken Lamanites, and Ammon showed them the way back to Zarahemla.

DISCUSSION QUESTIONS
1. What happened to some of King Noah's people?
2. What was King Noah's son's name? Was he good?
3. What did King Limhi tell his people to do so that God would help them?
4. How did the people escape?

RECIPE
(Take turns being the bad Lamanites who drink the drink and fall asleep, and King Limhi's people who escape.)
1 can (6 ounces) frozen grape juice concentrate
1/2 c. milk
1/2 c. ginger ale
1 1/2 c. vanilla ice cream

Put all ingredients into blender container. Cover and blend on high speed 30 seconds. Serve right away. If you have no blender, scoop the ice cream into a 2-quart jar with remaining ingredients. Cover tightly and shake. You can also beat in a large bowl with an egg beater.

Alma's Great Day Floats

Alma taught many people the gospel one day, and 204 of them were baptized that very day. We believe in being baptized by immersion. Immersion means going all the way under the water, like the ice cream in these floats.

STORY: Mosiah 17-18. After Alma escaped from King Noah, he repented of his sins and taught the people Abinadi's words. Because King Noah was still looking for him, during the day Alma hid by a pool called the Waters of Mormon.

Many people came to hear Alma speak. Alma taught them and told them to have faith in God. He told them to repent and be baptized and to serve God.

After the people listened to Alma speak, they clapped their hands with joy and said they wanted to be baptized. That day, 204 people were baptized in the Waters of Mormon and joined the church of Christ.

Alma ordained priests to teach the people and counseled them to teach nothing except the things that Alma had taught, which had been spoken by the prophets.

DISCUSSION QUESTIONS
1. Who was Alma?
2. In the day, where did Alma hide from King Noah?
3. When many people came to hear Alma, what did he tell them?
4. What did many of them do?
5. Are you excited to be baptized someday? Or if you have been baptized, tell about how you felt after you were baptized.

RECIPE
6 c. lemon-lime soda
4 scoops of strawberry sherbet (or any other flavor sherbet)

Pour 1 1/2 cups soda into tall glass. Drop a scoop of sherbet into soda and enjoy.

Alma the Younger's Angel Food Brittle Cake

When Alma the Younger was doing bad things, an angel came to him and his friends. The angel gave Alma the Younger the "brittle" truth. This scared him so much, he couldn't move.

STORY: Mosiah 27:10-19. Alma had a son named Alma the Younger. He and the four sons of King Mosiah made trouble for the church. They talked to many people secretly and tried to lead them away from the church. Some of the people followed him and the sons of King Mosiah. They left the church and became wicked.

One day, Alma the Younger and the four sons of King Mosiah went out to cause more problems for the church. Suddenly, an angel came to them and talked in a voice that sounded like thunder. It even caused the earth to shake! The young men fell to the ground because they were afraid and surprised. The angel asked why Alma the Younger was making trouble for the church, for it was the true church. He told Alma to go his way and to stop making trouble for the church. The angel then went away.

The young men knew that the angel had great power, and that power came from God. They knew that only God could make the earth tremble. Alma the Younger was so afraid that he couldn't speak or move, so the four sons of King Mosiah carried him to his father and explained what had happened.

When Alma's father heard this, he rejoiced. He knew his prayers had been answered. He and other church leaders fasted and prayed to make Alma the Younger speak and move again. After two days and nights, Alma the Younger stood up and said that he knew he had been doing wrong, but he had repented and God had forgiven him.

From that day forth, Alma the Younger and the sons of King Mosiah went to many cities, trying to undo the wrong they had done. As they did, they taught the people all that they had learned. They helped many people to believe in Jesus Christ.

DISCUSSION QUESTIONS
1. What was the name of Alma's son who made trouble for the church?
2. When they went to make trouble one day, what happened to them?
3. What happened to Alma the Younger?
4. What did his father do?
5. Did God forgive Alma the Younger? Why?
6. Does God forgive us when we do something wrong?

RECIPE
1 large container frozen whipped topping, thawed
1 c. crushed peanut brittle
1 large angel food cake
1 grated chocolate bar

Fold peanut brittle into whipped topping in a small mixing bowl. Frost top and sides of angel food cake. Sprinkle grated chocolate bar on top. Chill before serving.

Oreo Earthquake Escape Shake

When Alma the Younger and Amulek were taken to prison, they prayed for help. God helped them by giving them strength to break the ropes that bound them. Then He shook the earth and broke down the prison walls. This allowed Alma the Younger and Amulek to escape.

STORY: Mosiah 29:42 and Alma 4-14. Alma the Younger became the leader of the church, and he went to many cities teaching the gospel. In Ammonihah, nobody listened to him, and they spit on him and made him leave their city.

An angel came to Alma the Younger and told him to go back to that city. He obeyed the angel, and this time he entered the city from another way. He was very hungry when he arrived, and he asked a righteous man named Amulek for something to eat. An angel had told Amulek to help Alma the Younger, so Amulek took him to his home and gave him food.

Alma the Younger and Amulek went to speak to the people, and the Holy Ghost helped them. One of the men in the crowd was a wicked man named Zeezrom. Zeezrom tried to trick Amulek, but he could not. Soon Zeezrom began to tremble, for he knew he was wrong. Zeezrom realized that God was helping Alma the Younger and Amulek, and he asked them to teach him more.

Some believed Alma the Younger and Amulek's words, but most of the people were angry with them for telling them they were wicked. They tied them up and took them to the chief judge, who listened to the wicked people testify against them. The righteous people tried to help them, but the wicked people chased them out of the city. The wicked people threw the righteous women and children and the holy scriptures into a fire. Alma the Younger and Amulek were very sad and wanted to stop it, but they knew that God would bless the people who died in the fire.

They were then taken to prison, tied up, and beaten. They did not receive any food or water. Alma the Younger and Amulek prayed to God for strength, and God helped them break the ropes. Many who saw them do this were afraid, and they ran away. The earth began to shake, and the prison walls fell upon all the bad people. All of the people in the prison were killed except Alma the Younger and Amulek, who walked out of the prison unharmed.

DISCUSSION QUESTIONS
1. Who helped Alma the Younger in Ammonihah?
2. Who was Zeezrom?
3. What did the bad people do with Alma the Younger and Amulek when they didn't believe them?
4. How did Heavenly Father help them?
5. Does Heavenly Father have power to help us when we need it?

RECIPE
1 quart vanilla ice cream
3/4 c. milk
20 Oreo cookies (or any other chocolate sandwich cookie)

Set up Oreos in four piles of five on a plate or cookie sheet, so they look like pillars of a prison. As you tell the story, shake the plate so the Oreos fall. Have the children help put them in the blender with the other ingredients. Mix until smooth. Pour into glasses. Enjoy!

Ammon's Incredible, Edible Snowball Sheep

When Ammon volunteered to be a servant to King Lamoni, a Lamanite, the king put him to work caring for the sheep. Little did he know just how far Ammon would go to protect the king's sheep!

STORY: Alma 17:4-39. Ammon was one of the four sons of King Mosiah. He wanted to teach the Lamanites the gospel, but the Lamanites did not like the Nephites, so they tied Ammon up and took him to their king, Lamoni.

King Lamoni asked Ammon why he had come to his city. Ammon replied that he wanted to live with the Lamanites and be King Lamoni's servant. King Lamoni liked Ammon, so he gave Ammon the job of tending his sheep.

One day the sheep were drinking at the watering place, and some wicked Lamanites chased the sheep away. King Lamoni's servants were afraid because the king's sheep were gone. They knew the king would kill them if they lost the sheep. Ammon told them not to be afraid . Soon they found the sheep and brought them back to the water.

The wicked Lamanites came again to scatter the sheep, but Ammon told the other servants to surround the sheep. Then he went to the wicked Lamanites. The wicked Lamanites weren't afraid of Ammon. They thought they could kill him easily. But Ammon had the power of God. He threw stones with his sling and killed some of the Lamanites. The Lamanites tried to kill Ammon with their clubs, but he cut the arms off those who raised a club against him. The wicked men were amazed and afraid at Ammon's strength, so they ran away.

King Lamoni's servants gathered up the arms to show the king what Ammon had done.

DISCUSSION QUESTIONS
1. Who was Ammon?
2. Why did he go see the Lamanites when the Lamanites hated the Nephites?
3. What did they do to him when they found him?
4. Why did King Lamoni make Ammon his servant?
5. What happened while Ammon was watching the sheep? What did he do?
6. Would you have the courage to go and teach the gospel to a people that hated you?

RECIPE
4 white coconut "snowball" cupcakes
4 large marshmallows
12 small marshmallows
12 toothpicks
1/2 c. chocolate chips

Set up snowballs on individual plates and have the family assemble them. With a toothpick, stick one large marshmallow on the top. This will be the head. Break a toothpick in half and stick two small marshmallows onto the top of the head for ears. On the opposite side, add one more small marshmallow with a toothpick for the tail. Melt the chocolate chips and use a small paintbrush to "paint" on a sheep face with the melted chocolate.

Lamoni's Fry Bread

King Lamoni was a Lamanite. Today we call Lamanites Indians or Native Americans. Fry bread is a treat introduced to us by the Native Americans.

STORY: Alma 18-19. After King Lamoni's servants brought him the arms Ammon had cut off of the wicked Lamanites, he was very surprised. He didn't think a man could be so strong. He thought that Ammon was a god because of his great strength. Lamoni wanted to see Ammon, but he was afraid. When Ammon came to see the king, Lamoni didn't speak for one hour because he didn't know what to say to Ammon .

The Holy Ghost helped Ammon know what the king was thinking, and Ammon told the king that he was not God. He was just a man. King Lamoni asked Ammon what made him so strong. He wanted Ammon to teach him, and he told Ammon he would believe his words. Ammon taught Lamoni about God and Jesus. He told him the things that were written on the gold and brass plates.

King Lamoni believed Ammon's words, then prayed to God to be forgiven of his sins. He fell to the ground as if he were dead. The servants took Lamoni and laid him on a bed, where he lay for two days and two nights. Lamoni's wife asked Ammon to help, but Ammon knew the king wasn't dead. He knew that God was just helping Lamoni understand the truth. Ammon told Lamoni's wife that Lamoni would get up the next day, and she believed him.

The next day, just as Ammon had said, Lamoni stood up. He told the people he had seen Jesus Christ and he knew that God lived. Lamoni then taught his people about God. Many heard his words and believed, and many did not. Those who believed were baptized into the church.

DISCUSSION QUESTIONS
1. Why was Lamoni afraid to speak to Ammon?
2. Why did Lamoni fall to the ground?
3. What happened after Lamoni got up?
4. Do you know that Jesus Christ died for us and that God lives?
   (This question isn't to be answered aloud. Just ask everyone to think about it.)

RECIPE
(This recipe can work just as well using your own bread dough recipe.)
Vegetable oil
2 loaves frozen bread dough

Thaw the frozen dough in refrigerator overnight or at room temperature no longer than 6 hours. When the dough has thawed, heat oil to 375°. On lightly floured pastry cloth, roll out dough until 1 inch thick. Cut into squares or other shapes. Cook in oil for 1-2 minutes until brown. Turn over and cook other side. Dip in honey dip or top with any other topping like sugar, syrup, or jam.

Honey Dip
1/4 c. butter or margarine, softened
1/4 c. honey
Nutmeg (optional)

Beat butter and honey with fork in bowl. Sprinkle with a little nutmeg.

Sweet Is Keeping the Promise Cake

Even when their lives were threatened, the people of Ammon kept their promise not to fight. They dug a hole in the ground and buried their weapons, vowing not to use them again. With this treat, your family will also "dig" holes and pour in the condensed milk, then cover it up with whipped topping. Is there a promise you want to make as a family as you do this?

STORY: Alma 22-27. Lamoni's father, the king of all the Lamanites, joined the church and wanted all of his people to hear the gospel, so he sent King Mosiah's sons out to teach the people. He warned his people not to hurt them. Many Lamanites joined the church and didn't want to fight anymore, so they put their swords, spears, and other weapons into a pile. The righteous Lamanites that joined the church called themselves the people of Ammon.

Many Lamanites hated the people of Ammon and wouldn't believe in Jesus Christ, so they got ready to fight them. Ammon and his brothers saw the wicked Lamanites getting ready to fight, so they warned the king of what the Lamanites were planning to do.

The king gathered his people together and reminded them that they had once been wicked and had killed many people. But when they joined the church, they repented and were forgiven. He was afraid that if they killed again, they might not be forgiven. The people didn't want to kill anymore. They wanted to keep God's commandments and remain clean.

The king and his people decided not to fight the Lamanites. They threw their swords and other weapons in a hole and covered them up. They promised God they would never kill anyone or fight again, even if they lost their own lives.

Soon the wicked Lamanites came to fight, but the people of Ammon would not fight. Instead, they knelt down and began to pray. The wicked Lamanites killed many of the people of Ammon, but when they saw that the people of Ammon would not fight, they stopped killing them and threw their own weapons down. They also vowed not to pick them up again, and they repented and joined the people of Ammon. That day, more people joined the people of Ammon than were killed.

DISCUSSION QUESTIONS
1. After many of the Lamanites repented and joined the church, what did they

do with their weapons?

2. When they found out some wicked Lamanites were coming to fight them, what did they do?
3. What happened to many of the people?
4. How did some of the wicked Lamanites feel after they had killed some of the innocent people of Ammon? What did they do about it?
5. What promises have we made to Heavenly Father? Have we kept those promises?

RECIPE
Cake mix for German chocolate cake
14 oz. can of sweetened, condensed milk
One jar of caramel fudge topping
3 Skor or Heath candy bars, grated
Large container of whipped topping

Let whipped topping thaw in refrigerator for several hours. Bake German chocolate cake according to mix directions in a 13x9x2-inch pan and let cool for 20 minutes. With the handle of a wooden spoon, poke holes all over cake. Pour sweetened, condensed milk over holes. Next, pour in caramel fudge topping. Grate candy bars and fold into whipped topping, then spread mixture on top of cake. Refrigerate until ready to serve. Serves 12.

Title of Liberty Treats

Captain Moroni tore his coat, and on it he wrote about freedom. He caused the title of liberty to be hung all around the land to remind the people that freedom is a precious thing that they must always fight for.

STORY: Alma 43-48. Captain Moroni was a righteous leader of the Nephite armies. Amalickiah was the leader of the wicked people who wanted to kill the church leaders. Amalickiah wanted to be king of the Nephites and take away their freedom, so he told many lies to get people to help him. Unfortunately, many people believed him.

If Amalickiah became the king, he would not let them worship God or go to church, and the people would not have any freedom.

Captain Moroni was angry, for he didn't want this to happen to the people, so he tore his coat and wrote about freedom on one piece. He told his people to think of their freedom and to think of their families. Moroni used this piece of coat as a flag, and he put it on a pole. He called it the "title of liberty."

Moroni prayed for the church and the people and their homes. He showed the title of liberty to many people. In a loud voice, he asked the people to fight for their freedom. He told the people to obey God's commandments. If they did, God would help them be free.

After he said these things, many people promised that they would obey God's commandments and fight for freedom. Captain Moroni led an army to fight Amalickiah. Amalickiah saw that he couldn't win, so he and his people ran away, but Moroni's army chased them. Amalickiah left his army and ran away with a few of his men.

Moroni wanted the Nephites to remember the title of liberty, so he put a flag in every tower. Captain Moroni was a good man.

DISCUSSION QUESTIONS
1. Who was Moroni?
2. Who was Amalickiah?
3. Why did Moroni tear his coat and write on it?
4. What did he do with the coat?
5. Is freedom important? Why? Wouldn't it be easier to have someone make all of our decisions for us?
6. Discuss our pre-earth life and how we were part of the two-thirds of heaven that fought for freedom.
7. Do we have to fight for our freedom today? How?

RECIPE
2 rolls of fruit leather
4 strawberry candy sticks (or straight peppermint sticks)
Whipped cream

Cut fruit leather in half. Poke holes in the top left and bottom left corners of fruit leather with knife. Stick a candy stick through, so that it looks like a flag on a stick. Let everyone "fingerpaint" a message onto their "flag" with whipped cream.

Stripling Warrior Taffy

The 2,000 young stripling warriors had to be righteous and "pull together" to have Heavenly Father protect them. Your family will have to have faith and "pull together" as well to make this taffy! It will work if you follow the instructions and keep on pulling!

STORY: Alma 53-57. The Lamanites and Nephites had many wars. The Nephites fought hard to protect themselves and their families. They also fought to protect the people of Ammon, who had taken an oath not to shed any blood.

As the Nephites fought, the people of Ammon saw that the armies needed help. They wanted to help fight for their country, but Helaman, a son of Alma the Younger, told the people of Ammon to keep their promise.

The people of Ammon had many young sons who were strong, brave, and righteous. These sons had not promised God they wouldn't fight. These 2,000 sons met together and promised that they would fight for their country. They called themselves Nephites. Their mothers taught them to have faith in God, so they were not afraid to fight. They asked Helaman to be their leader.

When Helaman led the young warriors to fight, they came upon the Nephites and Lamanites fighting. The Lamanites were winning. Helaman's army helped the Nephites. Helaman gave orders and the young men obeyed, fighting bravely. At the end of the fight, the Nephites, with the young warriors' help, had won.

One thousand Nephite soldiers were dead, and Helaman was afraid many of his young men had been killed. But although he found all of the young men sick or hurt, not one of them was dead. They had faith that God would bless them, and He did.

DISCUSSION QUESTIONS
1. Who were the parents of the 2,000 stripling warriors?
2. Why did the stripling warriors decide to fight for freedom with Helaman and help the Nephites?
3. After the battle, how many of the young men were killed?
4. Why did God help them?

RECIPE
2 c. sugar
1 c. light corn syrup
1 c. water
3/4 tsp. salt
2 Tbsp. butter or margarine
1/4 tsp. peppermint extract, or other extract flavor
Food coloring

In a 2-quart saucepan, combine sugar, corn syrup, water, and salt. Stir constantly as you cook over medium heat until sugar dissolves; butter the sides of the pan as it cooks. Continue cooking on medium heat WITHOUT STIRRING for 40 minutes until it reaches the hard ball stage (265°).

At that time, remove from heat and stir in butter, flavoring, and food color. Butter a 15x10x1-inch pan and pour in mixture, allowing it to cool about 25 minutes or until you can handle it.

Now comes the fun part: With well-buttered hands, pull taffy until it is difficult to pull. Cut this piece into fourths, then pull each piece into a long strand 1/2 inch thick. Cut taffy into bite-size pieces with buttered scissors or a sharp, buttered knife, and wrap in waxed paper. Makes 1 1/2 pounds.

Samuel the Lamanite's Rice Crispie Wall

Samuel the Lamanite stood on a Nephite wall to prophesy and to tell the people to repent. Make your own wall with this treat, throw M&M "stones" at it, then eat it down!

STORY: Helaman 13-16. After many years, most of the Nephites became wicked. They didn't obey God anymore. But the Lamanites became righteous, and they obeyed God's commandments.

Samuel the Lamanite went to Zarahemla to teach the Nephites. He tried to get them to repent. But the Nephites wouldn't listen to Samuel, and they cast him out of their city.

As Samuel was returning to his own city, the Lord told him to go back to Zarahemla to prophesy and teach the people. Because the Nephites wouldn't let him into their city, he stood on the wall and told the Nephites that God had sent him. He told them to repent and believe in Jesus Christ. If they would not repent, God would punish them.

He also told the people of many things that were going to happen. He said Jesus Christ would be born in five years. The people in America would know when Jesus Christ was born near Jerusalem, for on the night before he was born, it would not grow dark at night. It would be light for a day, a night, and another day. The people would also see a new star, and then they would know that Jesus Christ was born.

Samuel also told about Jesus' death and said that it would be dark for three days in America. He said that the sun, moon, and stars wouldn't shine. There would be fierce storms and the earth would shake. Mountains would fall down and cities would be destroyed.

Many people were angry with Samuel. They didn't believe him, so they threw rocks and shot arrows at him. God protected Samuel and wouldn't let the arrows and rocks hurt him. The people even tried to catch him, but he jumped off the wall and ran away to his own land. He never came back to the Nephites.

Some of the Nephites believed Samuel, and they repented and were baptized.

DISCUSSION QUESTIONS
1. Why did Samuel the Lamanite stand on the Nephites' wall?
2. What did Samuel tell them?
3. What did the wicked Nephites do to Samuel?
4. Did anyone believe Samuel? What did the belivers do?

RECIPE
4 c. crispy rice cereal
3 c. marshmallows
1/4 c. butter
3 Tbsp. peanut butter
1 jar caramel sauce
M&Ms or other candies

Melt butter on low heat, then add marshmallows. When the marshmallows are melted, stir in peanut butter. Add cereal and stir until well blended. Turn out into a square pan prepared with non-stick cooking spray, and spread smooth. Let cool for 20 minutes. Cut into squares. On a cookie sheet or cake platter, stack 3 squares for the wall's "base," adding caramel sauce between squares and on top. Now add more squares on top, drizzling more caramel sauce. Do it one more time, or until out of squares.

As you tell the story, have the kids throw M&Ms or other candies at the wall at the point when the wicked people threw stones and shot arrows at Samuel. Eat the wall down and enjoy!

Cake of the Angels

After Jesus was crucified, he visited America and blessed the children. Then angels came down from heaven and blessed the children.

STORY: 3 Nephi 12-26. After three days, it became light and the earthquakes stopped. The people stopped crying and began praising God. Many people were near the temple when they heard a voice coming from heaven. It was a soft voice, but it seemed to touch their very souls. They all listened, for it was Heavenly Father's voice and He said, "Behold my Beloved Son, in whom I am well pleased, in whom I have glorified my name—hear ye him."

Jesus came down in a white robe and said, "I am Jesus Christ." The people fell to the earth and bowed down to him. But Jesus told them to arise. He showed them the marks of the nails in his hands and feet, so that they might know he was Jesus. He then let them feel the holes in his hands and feet.

Jesus then gave Nephi and some other men the power to baptize the people, and he showed them the right way to baptize. He taught all the people the gospel and told them to repent and be baptized. He chose twelve leaders for his church and gave them the priesthood, then explained to the people the power he had given them. He also told them many other things and healed the sick, the blind, and the deaf. Then he blessed each of the children.

Suddenly the people looked up and saw angels come down from heaven to bless the children. Then Jesus taught the people about the sacrament.

The people loved Jesus. They wanted him to stay with them, but Jesus had finished his work in America and went back to his Heavenly Father.

DISCUSSION QUESTIONS
1. What did Jesus do when he came to America?
2. What did the angels do when they came down from heaven?
3. Would you have liked to be here when Jesus came down? Why?

RECIPE
1 1/4 c. sugar
1/2 c. water
6 egg yolks
6-12 thin slices angel food cake
2 c. bite-size pieces ripe fresh pineapple
1 container frozen whipped topping or whipped cream

Boil sugar and water in medium saucepan until sugar dissolves, then cover pan and cool slightly. Put egg yolks in medium mixing bowl and beat constantly as you slowly pour the syrup mixture into the yolks.

Cook this mixture in a medium saucepan on low heat, stirring constantly until thickened, but not boiling. (This may take up to 15 minutes.) Strain and let the sauce cool, stirring occasionally. Do not refrigerate.

Place cake pieces on individual plates, spooning pineapple lightly over cake and ladling the sauce on top. Add a dollop of whipped topping and serve.

PEACE IN AMERICA SUNDAES

When Jesus visited America, he taught the people that the only way to have peace was to share. That way no one was poor and went without food or clothing. Your family will discover that they'll be a lot happier if they share what they have, for they'll receive many blessings.

STORY: 4 Nephi 1. After Jesus left them, all the people, Lamanites and Nephites, joined the church. They shared with each other, and no one was rich and no one was poor. The church leaders performed many miracles. They healed people who were sick or hurt, and helped the deaf and blind people to hear and to see. They also brought dead people back to life.

God blessed the people, so they were strong and worked hard. They built many new cities, and rebuilt Zarahemla and other cities that had been burned.

The people obeyed God's commandments and loved each other and didn't fight. They married and had many children. Because they obeyed God's commandments and helped each other, there was not a happier people to be found anywhere.

DISCUSSION QUESTIONS
1. Why was there peace in America?
2. What is peace?
3. Would it be a good thing to have in our home? Why?
4. How can we have peace in our home?

RECIPE
Caramel topping
Hot fudge topping
Chopped nuts
Whipped cream
Maraschino cherries
Vanilla ice cream
Other toppings as desired

Give each family member a topping for their own. They can choose to share with everyone, or keep it all to themselves. After you make and eat your sundaes, ask if it is better to keep something all to oneself or to share with others. Why?

Proud Puffs

After Christ visited America, the people lived for many years in peace. Then the people started to become proud of their clothes and material things. They became "puffed up" and proud. They felt that material goods were more important than their eternal well-being.

STORY: 4 Nephi 1:23-45. Many years went by, and the people were happy and lived in peace. They shared all they had with each other. But then the people became very rich. They became "puffed up" and proud of their clothes and houses and worldly possessions, and they didn't share anymore.

Some of them didn't believe in Jesus Christ anymore, so they started their own churches for their own gain. After a while, only a few people believed in Jesus. All the others, both Lamanites and Nephites, were vain because they had so many riches.

DISCUSSION QUESTIONS
1. Why did some of the Nephites become wicked again?
2. What did the people start to forget when they got too many material things?
3. Do we sometimes get caught up in wanting things?
4. How do we stop ourselves from doing this?

RECIPE
Vegetable oil
3/4 c. milk
1/2 c. sugar
1/4 c. oil
2 eggs
3 tsp. baking powder
1/4 tsp. salt
1/2 tsp. mace
2 1/2 c. flour
1/2 c. currants or raisins (optional)
1/4 c. sugar

1/2 tsp. cinnamon
1/4 tsp. nutmeg

Before mixing ingredients, heat oil (2-3 inches in a pan) to 375º. In large mixing bowl beat milk, 1/2 cup sugar, 1/4 cup oil, eggs, baking powder, salt, mace, and 1 cup of the flour on low speed. Beat on medium speed, scraping bowl occasionally, for 2 minutes. Gently stir in remaining flour and the currants or raisins.

Using a teaspoon, drop dough into hot oil and turn puffs as they rise. Cook for 2 to 2 1/2 minutes on each side or until golden brown. Drain on paper towels.

Mix 1/4 cup sugar with the cinnamon and nutmeg. Roll puffs in the mixture. Puffs may also be topped with honey, jam, pudding, or any other toppings you might enjoy.

Mormon's Hope Swirl Bread

Mormon tried to make several treaties with the Lamanites. He hoped that they all could live in peace, the Nephites and the Lamanites together, like this swirl bread. The filling and the bread make each other taste better.

STORY: Mormon 1:47-7:18. Ammaron was a righteous man who wrote on the gold plates about his people. He didn't want the wicked people to find the plates, so he hid them. He told Mormon, a righteous ten-year-old boy, where he had hidden them. Ammaron told Mormon to get the plates when he was 24 years old and write on them the things he had observed about his people.

When Mormon was 15 years old, Jesus visited him and Mormon knew of his goodness. Mormon wanted the people to repent and believe in Jesus Christ, but the people were too wicked and began to fight each other again. Because Mormon was a large man at 16 years old, the people of Nephi asked him to be the leader of their armies.

The people fought for many years, but Mormon knew the Nephites couldn't win the war. They were so wicked that God wouldn't help them anymore.

Mormon took the plates from where Ammaron had hidden them and wrote to the Lamanites. He urged them to repent and be baptized, and he also wrote that God loved the Lamanites. Mormon wrote that he was sad that they were wicked. He hoped they would believe in God someday, and they could all live in peace.

DISCUSSION QUESTIONS
1. Who was Ammaron?
2. Who did Ammaron tell about the gold plates?
3. What did Mormon write on the plates?
4. What would have happened if the prophets hadn't written down their histories, thoughts, feelings, and experiences?
5. Do you think it's important to keep a journal? Why?

RECIPE
1 package active dry yeast
1/4 c. warm water (105-115º)
3/4 c. lukewarm milk
1/2 c. butter, softened

3 eggs
1/4 c. sugar
1/2 tsp. salt
4 1/2 -5 c. flour
Walnut or Apple Filling (recipe below)
Powdered sugar icing (from Sword of Laban Breadstick Treats)

Preheat oven to 350°. Dissolve yeast in warm water in large bowl. Stir in milk, butter, eggs, sugar, salt, and 3 cups flour and beat until smooth. If dough is still runny, stir in enough remaining flour to make dough stiffer and easy to handle.

On lightly floured surface, knead dough until smooth and elastic (about 5 minutes). Place in greased bowl and cover, letting it rise in warm place until doubled, 1 to 1 1/2 hours.

Punch dough down and divide into halves. On lightly floured surface, roll each half into a rectangle, 15x12 inches. Spread half the filling over each rectangle and roll up tightly, beginning at 15-inch side. Seal dough and filling well by pinching edges of dough together. Stretch to make rolls even with each other.

Coil rolls into snail shapes on greased cookie sheets with the pinched sides down. Cover; let rise until double, about 1 hour. Bake 35-45 minutes. Bread should be golden brown. Drizzle with powdered sugar icing (from Sword of Laban Breadstick Treats).

Walnut or Apple Filling
2 1/2 cups finely chopped walnuts (or finely chopped apples if you prefer)
1 c. packed brown sugar
1/3 c. butter, softened
1 egg
2 tsp. cinnamon
1/2 tsp. nutmeg (if using apples)

Mix all ingredients.

Book of Mormon Jello

Moroni promises that if we "devour" the Book of Mormon prayerfully, we will know of its truthfulness. Urge your family to devour these treats, then work on reading the Book of Mormon until it's completed.

STORY: Mormon 6-8, Moroni 10:1, 4. Many years passed, and Mormon grew old. He hid most of the gold plates in the Hill Cumorah so the Lamanites wouldn't find them and destroy them. He gave a few plates to his son, Moroni, so he could finish the record.

There was a great battle, and all of the Nephites were killed except Moroni. Moroni hid so he wouldn't be killed, and he wrote on the gold plates what had happened to his people. He also wrote about things Jesus had taught them— how we should bless the sacrament, baptize and confirm people, and many other things.

Moroni also wrote a promise to the Lamanites and everyone who reads the book. He said that we should read the Book of Mormon and pray to know if it is true. He promised us that if we have faith, the Holy Ghost will tell us the Book of Mormon is true. (Read the promise in Moroni 10: 3-4.)

After Moroni finished writing on the plates, he hid them in a stone box on a hill and covered the box with a big rock. Hundreds of years later, Moroni appeared as an angel to Joseph Smith and showed him where to find the plates.

DISCUSSION QUESTIONS

1. Who was Moroni?
2. What did Moroni write on the plates?
3. What did Moroni do with the plates?
4. What was the promise he made about the Book of Mormon?
5. After you read the Book of Mormon, will you try his promise out?

RECIPE

2 pkgs. (4-serving size) lemon Jello
1 pkg. cream cheese
1/2 bag mini marshmallows
Container of Cool Whip, thawed
1 can crushed pineapple
1/2 c. coconut

Mix 1 box of the Jello with hot and cold water as directed on package. Pour into 13x9x2-inch pan. Pinch off small dobs of cream cheese and drop all over unset Jello. Drop marshmallows onto Jello. Chill until set, about 3 hours. Mix other box of Jello as directed and pour on top of set Jello. Chill until set. In mixing bowl, gently mix whipped topping with pineapple and coconut. Spread this mixture on top of set Jello. Cut into squares, so that they look like little "golden plates."

Testimony Root Beer Floats

President Ezra Taft Benson gave a powerful message about the importance of reading the Book of Mormon. Share it with your family, then liken what he said to the root beer floats. The ice cream is you, the root beer is the Book of Mormon. The more you read (or immerse yourself in) the Book of Mormon, the more your testimony (the foam) will grow.

MESSAGE

President Ezra Taft Benson said:

[The Book of Mormon] helps us draw nearer to God. Is there not something deep in our hearts that longs to draw nearer to God, to be more like Him in our daily walk, to feel His presence with us constantly? If so, then the Book of Mormon will help us do so more than any other book.

It is not just that the Book of Mormon teaches us truth, though it indeed does that. It is not just that the Book of Mormon bears testimony of Christ, though it indeed does that, too. But there is something more. There is a power in the book which will begin to flow into your lives the moment you begin a serious study of the book. You will find the power to avoid deception. You will find the power to stay on the strait and narrow path. The scriptures are called "the words of life" (see D&C 84:85), and nowhere is that more true than it is of the Book of Mormon. When you begin to hunger and thirst after those words, you will find life in greater and greater abundance. (*Ensign*, Nov. 1986, p. 7.)

DISCUSSION QUESTIONS

1. What is a testimony?
2. How do we feel it? What does it feel like?
3. What are some things that might make a testimony get weak?
4. How can we help our testimonies to grow?

RECIPE
4 scoops vanilla ice cream
6 to 8 cups root beer

Put ice cream in a glass. Pour root beer on top and see the foam rise up!